Lunar Rainbow

New writing from
Artemesia Arts
poetry competition
2024

MOSAÏQUEPRESS

First published in 2024

MOSAÏQUE PRESS
Registered office:
70 Priory Road
Kenilworth, Warwickshire
CV8 1LQ

All poems are the Copyright © of their Authors

The right of the copyright holders to be identified as the authors of this work has been asserted in accordance with Section 77 of the Copyright, Designs and Patents Act 1998.

Cover illustration: *Horizon #6* (dye on silk)
Copyright © René Shoemaker 2024

ISBN 978-1-906852-69-6

Foreword

It's traditional to say how hard a job it's been, and with such strong poems I could say this and be believed. But after my initial selection I realised the task wasn't to find the 'best' poems so much as to identify my favourites, so the process became hugely enjoyable.

My approach was to re-read them all – often when they least expected it – and notice which ones I most relished going back to. The longer this process went on, the more enjoyable it became.

So the prize-winners and the highly commendeds are the poems that sang to me, or sang the sweetest. And while appreciation of poetry is always personal, I'm confident these poems will give pleasure to a wide range of readers.

Matt Harvey
May 2024

Matt Harvey is a performance poet, lyricist and columnist, well-known to BBC Radio 4 listeners from his own *One Night Stanza* series and as a regular poet on *Saturday Live*.

Describing himself as an enemy of all that's difficult and upsetting, Matt was host of Radio 4's comedy-infused poetry cabaret *Wondermentalist*. He was also appointed official Wimbledon Championship Poet in 2010.

Matt has had a wealth of collections published. Described as "brilliant" by the *New Yorker*, Matt is a poetry columnist for several publications including the *Guardian*.

www.mattharvey.co.uk.

Contents

Winner
6   Glen Wilson
7   Setting Bones

Runners-up
8   **Denise O'Hagan** The Maid Awakens at 5am Marseille, November 1829
9   **Derek Sellen** The Strangeness of Water

Highly Commended
10 **Gary Day** Anne Brontë's Grave: St Mary's Church, Scarborough
11 **Sujatha Menon** Cytoskeleton of a Spell
12 **Erica Jane Morris** Further Failings
13 **Mark Totterdell** Shiver
14 **Rod Whitworth** Lake

Selected
15 **Philip Bellamy** Whodunnit
16 **Alice Brooker** Musings in Vitruvian
17 **Lesley Cooke** Still Breathing
18 **Gary Day** White Phosphorous
19 **Francesca Duffield** Home Thoughts from Abroad
20 **Claudi Farese** Black Dog Follows You Home
21 **Tessa Foley** Breath
22 **Andrew George** Tricolore Heute
23 **Eileen Anne Gordon** Dealing with Monsters
24 **Kate Grattan** Before the Moon
25 **Pam Job** Aide Memoire

26 **Ben Keatinge** Rossini in Skopje
27 **Sue Kindon** A Proverbial Example
28 **Sue Kindon** The Very Grey Area of Suburbain Zebras
29 **Bridget Khurshead** Last Day in the Mountains
30 **Frank Lowry** Attic
31 **Kristen Mears** Tennis Lessons
32 **Sujatha Menon** Mimicry in G Minor
33 **Mili McCoy** Blush
34 **Erica Jane Morris** Flies
35 **Ansuya Patel** Abecedarian of a Train Journey
36 **Geoff Petty** Crank
37 **Anthony Powers** Wearing a Poem
38 **Estelle Price** Metaphor or Lessons Learnt in the Middle of the Night, St Albans
40 **Martin Rieser** A Stitch in Time
41 **Gloria Sanders** Drawing Life
42 **Korrin Smith Whitehouse** Knowing Nothing
43 **Jackie Skingley** Chiaroscuro
44 **Jackie Skingley** Muttrah Souq Remembered
45 **Sally Spiers** Bonxies
46 **Sally Stanford** Rainforest
47 **Marcus Tickner** Christmas Lights in January
48 **Christian Ward** Beetle Translations
50 **Judith Wozniak** Johannes Could Turn Oil into Light
52 **Jill Zhao** Deadman's Ponds

55 The poets
61 About the cover illustrator
63 Afterword from Artemesia Arts

About the winner...

Irish poet Glen Wilson says winning the Artemesia Arts poetry competition was "a massive honour". For his winning poem, 'Setting Bones', he drew inspiration from the work of First World War field hospital volunteers Anne Acheson and Elinor Hallé, who used their sculpting and designing skills to create plaster of Paris casts to treat soldiers' broken bones.

"I was intrigued by the various aspects of the arts, healing, war and identity and how they all interacted and aligned with each other when I was creating this poem. It was a challenge to take something fractured and build it anew," Glen said.

Glen has built up a collection of accolades on both sides of the Irish sea over the past five years. His poem 'Angelshare' appeared on the inaugural Poetry Jukebox at the Crescent Arts Centre in Belfast. He also appears on film narrating poems he was was commissioned to write for the Northern Ireland Football Association to write poems for the Northern Ireland Football Association.

Glen lives with his wife and two children in Portadown, Co Armagh. He works as a civil servant and is Worship Leader at St Mark's Church of Ireland Portadown. He studied English and Politics at Queens University Belfast and has a post-graduate diploma in Journalism studies from the University of Ulster.

Glen Wilson

Setting Bones

I watch walking sculptures
peeled back in part   and some in whole

to their first drafts   elementary
sketches of anatomy.

Whispered words fill the air
from the   half-jawed wounded.

I carry the one-sided weight
of conversation

and fill in the blanks
and change   the gauze dressing

on sutures and sentences
treating the boy   and the man.

I see formative art in the tangle
of red   gossamer threads

how clothed in white
and angled divine

a withered hand
extended out in hope

will grow to the healing
given time

and the scaffold embrace
of plaster of Paris.

They will leave
like all muses do
their step quicker
          their limp less

each like Prometheus
on a promise.

Denise O'Hagan

The Maid Awakens at 5am
Marseille, November 1829

   —and again I fall
into that flat blue hour before dawn when
the world, and all in it, are poised on the precipice
of a new day, the curtains hanging more heavily
than usual, folding shadow in brocaded columns,
as the dull brass curtain rail lies waiting
and the tabby's ears are pricked,
even in slumber. This moment
has lasted for centuries.

   Later, the light will lick the gap
under my door golden, illumine the sloping
attic roof, my starched white apron folded neatly
on the back of the wooden chair, cap dangled
at its corner and I'll breathe the chill
from my cupped hands, slowly rake the ashes
from last night's fire, get the water boiling
before the family arises. But first—

   I will open my bedroom window
to that stippled silver veil of mist rising like steam
from the rooftops, drifting free and unencumbered
over the pleated fields of newly planted wheat
to where they say the sea is, and other places
I cannot even imagine.

   Only then
harbouring the kernel of that vast freedom
like a jewel to my chest, will I prepare
to secrete myself into the blurred margins
of other people's days,
     one more time.

RUNNER-UP
ARTEMESIA ARTS
POETRY
COMPETITION
2024

Derek Sellen

The Strangeness of Water

Yes, water's a strange thing,
        a hard problem to solve,
  permeating the impermeable,
    slinking behind plaster
        and rising through floorboards,
    a monotone clink
      in a bucket
    or a gush under the door,
   tame from the tap,
wild
   when it smashes the esplanade,
      sly
and untraceable
    when it seeps,
dribbling bubbles of doubt into the mind –
      fountain of light,
        dank well,
   it births and it drowns,
     cleanses
        and smirches,
     freezes and thaws
        and disappears into
          air,
      quenches
        and
          thirsts,
     for land to swallow,
      for the return
        of those
          who once
            belonged to water,
              hugging us like family
                if we swim
                  or if we
                    fall,
                  calling
                    in wet syllables
                      to our aquatic core

Gary Day

Anne Brontë's Grave: St Mary's Church, Scarborough

At first glance it looks neglected,
Tufts of grass and the brittle stalks
Of some dead flower, yet this is the one
They come to see. Is it a reverence

For the written word that draws them here?
Or because it's on the tourist trail, along with
The Spa, the Italian Gardens and the Castle,
Still defying its own demise?

Little offerings adorn the base:
A feather, a bracelet, the head
Of a violet and a scattering of pebbles.
The gravestone is flecked with white;

Salt air has corroded the copperplate
Epitaph. Its looping letters have lost
Their curls; now there are spaces where
There were words. Wind and rain

Have blurred the relief of a draped urn
Resting on two novels recording, like
Those of her sisters, the tide of history
Rising in provincial lives.

Emily and Charlotte are together
At Haworth but Anne lies alone,
Except for her unfathomable
Visitors and the sea singing to her bones.

Sujatha Menon

Cytoskeleton of a Spell

I

Prevents worn syllables collapsing into a hex/ hexoplasm
spreads like a boil burst with an infected tooth/ the pulp of
the tooth contains the genetic code for extra-sensory
salivation/ the salivary gland blooms with poison/
the poison is unctuous and coats the spell.

II

Enables spell division through the assisted movement
of love towards hate/ hatefulness breeds intent to forage
for fools that nourish the tongue/ the tongue is forked
but not like a snake's/ snake oil is a poor man's poison.

III

Aids in snail motility and co-operation/ snails are
co-opted by a system they serve, even in their struggle
against it/ 'struggle & bubble' is a basic spell/
but not one which produces much poison.

VI

Enhances signalling through spell receptors/
reception can be interrupted in areas with poor
telekinesis/ when evil is telekinetic,
it can move monsters from under the bed/
the ones that slip poison in your morning coffee.

V

Maintains spell shape in the presence of benevolent
forces/ forcing the break of a spell creates cracks
in the cauldron/ the cauldron is built to withstand
blessings but not the torturous whimper of grace/
there is no pity in poison.

Erica Jane Morris

Further Failings

I failed at cartwheels, backwards
head over heels. I failed to see
the amoeba, killed a water flea
with petroleum jelly. I failed to read
inside my head. The lead in my pencil
slid out. My ant farm flooded.
I failed to save money, backpack
around Peru. I failed to be absorbed
by Austen. I failed to light
a firelighter, was asked to leave
the choir. I refused to stand up
and sit down. I missed the last train,
forgot to post my Christmas cards.
I failed at mountain pose,
dead dog. I forgot to be mindful,
failed at nasal breathing. I lost myself
in the Brecon Beacons. I dropped out
of ballet, failed to learn the acoustic guitar.
My laugh was too loud. I failed
at tripping. He wrote his number
on a ten-pound note. I spent it. I broke
the handle on a pasta machine, failed
to find the inner piece. The zip stuck
on my onesie. I woke up
in a breakout room. I planted thistles.
I've never had a PB, positive splits
made me sick. I burnt the scallops.
My bag for life perished. I failed
to delegate, circulate, tone
my midriff. I crocheted treble, not
half treble double treble. I unravelled.
My sourdough starter grew mould.
I failed to give up my seat. I failed
at grieving. My hair went green. I never
found my double. I failed to tap my Oyster
and retweet. I failed at stitching
patchwork bunting. I didn't trim
the wick. My lipstick melted.
I shrunk my wedding dress. I failed
to sleep.

HIGHLY COMMENDED
ARTEMESIA ARTS POETRY COMPETITION 2024

Mark Totterdell

Shiver

The redwings have brought the darkness and the cold
down from the north. Each carried a small sliver
of ice in its beak. Their shrill sounds as they called
each other in the night could make you shiver.

One's here in the garden's berry tree, alone,
gorging itself on all that is ripe and red.
Above its bright eye you see the pale drawn line,
under its wing the staining as if it bled.

It flew in a flock that specked the winter sky
like the dark feathers on its delicate breast.
You fancy that you can feel the unhealed scar
in its small heart where it broke off from the rest.

What you need most is for it to fly off now,
find its companions out in the endless blue,
while you'll continue to shun all company
until this foul thing has run its course in you.

Rod Whitworth

Lake

It is not a place where you would graze sheep
or play a game of tennis
or teach a child to walk.

It is not suitable for use as a cape
or as a television screen
or for making into cutlery.

It never answers to your call
nor tells you bedtime stories
nor plays the nose flute.

It would be no use as a parachute
or a scythe
or a tuning fork.

You couldn't take it out to tea
or enrol it in a choir.
You would struggle to write on it.

But see how it holds that mountain
and the nearer oak woods
in its frosty reflecting blue.

Philip Bellamy

Whodunnit

Everything seems to fit on the page:
The Colonel, the country house, the poisoned chalice.
But then you begin to question things a little too closely.
Why was the Will altered so often?
Did all the relatives really have a motive?
Why did they all turn up to dinner on the same night?
You get in a pickle about red herrings,
Suspect foul play from the author,
Want the detective to ditch his sidekick 200 pages earlier,
Be able to recognise the killer by Chapter 4,
Get his grey cells working before the second slaying.
You suspect everyone and no-one:
Smirk when the Butler drops his tray,
Frown when the Housemaid enters with an alibi,
Are agape when the Vicar prays for forgiveness.
You want to dig the dirt on the Gardener,
Catch the philandering son in flagrante,
Examine the Doctor's dubious credentials,
Question the Chauffeur about his breaks,
Decipher the Secretary's sinister shorthand,
Ask the Cook about her Goose.

When it's time for the denouement,
You feel clueless, a dupe, a silly ass,
A hapless victim of paper-thin evidence,
Left with an ending that hangs
Heavily on your shoulders.
But, slowly, you realise that there's less here
Than meets the eye;
That logic tells you the plot makes no sense,
That the flaws are too great, the explanations too wild,
The murderer too unlikely, the outcome too preposterous,
The narrator just too unreliable.
So, you scornfully cast it aside,
Call it a criminal waste of time,
And swiftly move on to the next one,
Ready to go through the trial once again.

Alice Brooker

Musings in Vitruvian

Limbs sum up something far
larger than a soul, I am whole

in my multiples, incapable of coordination
down to the tongue, connecting dots
    of
        speech

without teeth, just wingspan and hand

over ear can you hear this? There's
more than me to know, conceive my

cacophony of fingers and toes and
corporeal joy, a boy the width

of a forest, height of a nothing–
knight me as this paradox of human

circle, learn me with a sun inside.
Unburnt and ungendered and

try believing this belly is less than home–
breathing–protruding
               out at each scrutinising eye

I dare you to say I take up
    space,
to call me woman and name it waste.

Still Breathing

A giant's sword lies across the stream.
Three oaks jewel the hilt, fenced
by the shining cross-guard of running water.
While the sword lives, the giant
will not die from his wounds.

As he breathes out, trees gleam
with new leaves. Acorns form.
As he breathes in, leaves fall:
jewels look dull for a season.
As he breathes out, cattle find shade
beneath the oaks and the wild rose blooms.

As he breathes in,
blackberries and chestnuts appear,
food for the creatures living below.
People tramp the length of the blade,
keeping it sharp. Rain-filled dips

reveal the bright steel beneath the clay.
Its sheath lies in hedges of hawthorn
and honeysuckle; as the giant breathes in,
hips and haws ripen, food for birds
living on the edge.

The bridge over the stream is a portal,
a doorway to the giant's hilltop bed.
His hand lies not on his sword
but by his side, resting from strife.
Blood trickles from the wound in his heart

and feeds the stream, the three oaks,
the buried blade, the trees of his cloak.
He and his sword guard this corner
of the Earth, awaiting the next battle.
Those who fight for the way of truth
cannot return unchanged.

Gary Day

White Phosphorous

At the first sign of invasion
Trees bite off their tongues,
Flowers retreat underground;
Then the bombardment of snow.

Missiles rip through the air
Buildings fall to their knees,
Soldiers scuttle over the wreckage,
Hunting things to kill.

There is no defence against
The advancing snow. It
Overwhelms valleys, hills
And fields. There is beauty

In their obliteration. Viewers
Are warned they may find
Some of the following scenes
Upsetting. They watch

Anyway. What they see
Will mostly be forgotten
By bedtime. When they
Open their doors tomorrow

They will not be shot.
A conceptual artist declares wastelands
To be the only places in a city
Without definition. A tank

Clambers over what was a home,
A school or a hospital, its proboscis
Twitching. The stalk of an arm
Pushes up through the debris.

Trees are passing messages again,
Flowers are on the move. The snow
Is in retreat, except in the city where
it smells of garlic and falls as fire.

Francesca Duffield

Home Thoughts from Abroad

A childish finger trembles
on her cracked lip,
stopping a tear, hushing herself
into silence,
against the roar of Paris

she knows his gaze that once pierced her,
strays towards the doorway,
his impatience burns high
in the oxygen of the open window

in a moment, she will rise slowly,
she will leave the words of the dead poet
shut in the dark wardrobe,
drowned out by the chattering empty hangers
for, once this cramped room is vacant and swept clean,
the crumpled bed stripped bare,
the key swinging slowly on its brass hook

there will be no souvenirs to take home, to cling to
on the treacherous ship
waiting for the white battlements of home
in the mist,
green eyes fixed on grey water,
her sea-cold hands will be empty with
nothing left to be broken

Claudi Farese

Black Dog Follows You Home

To survive
Bring the black dog walk
Ask for sticks, in the park
To build a fort:
A rib for every cage,
Till its fur shines
Sleek and saturated.

Then, cool down.
Run a bath,
Recite poetry on your knees,
Every syllable like the ultimate call.
If Dog needs to eat your heart,
Offer verses in slam
And diary scraps.

Appeased of woe,
Lull him to artificial sounds
Until he sleeps alone.
Let the blue of night
Explode,
Offer stars in return -
Dance dance dance
Shake the devil from your back

Toss and turn
Shield its nasty claws
From your stomach, chest and heart
Dream in the full dark
Picture Schrödinger's cat
Nor alive, nor passed
Until Imbolc -
Then ask for light,
Walk through spring's gates
Till it melts the ice.

Breath

Though it's so many years ago,
Do we remember high, green air?
That scattered dawn, when we got out of bed
before the adults
and walked a whispering, empty road
so many gags and coughs ago.

There was a fine new-minted sun,
pebbles like from a jewellery box
all sticking, stacked right down the lane
before a soul
could watch us pick them up and bounce them
through the shards of air onto the rocks.

There were tall, sweet waving arms and
unrealistic, nearby peaks and we
were way too young to hear them speak
before we soured,
but we could taste the difference of this breath,
The cleanest deep.

On the trip-trap, furious white rolling underneath,
We breathed and hurt our lungs, our tongues,
our teeth, our bones,
before we found,
something so pure could only be inhaled
piece by piece.

Far from the city soft and poisoned puffs,
the toughest bludgeon of wholesome breeze
still maybe births the blinding grass and trees
After we left –
back in search of contaminated and
Life-shortening breath.

Tricolore Heute

Où-es tu maintenant, Didier?
Thick black curls and shining leather jacket.
The windswept backdrop of old La Rochelle,
Ton vélo, and your friends always ready
To *allons à la discothèque,*
Jouons au tennis de table.
Und wie geht es dir Günther?
Clipped blonde hair and trim moustache,
Issuing directions.
Nehmen Sie yet
Die erste straße links
For Wismar's busy station?

Where are you all,
Beautiful heroes of
Language textbooks?
Have you settled to retirement,
Exchanging post cards with your English colleagues,
Tina and Keith from Ramsgate, Kent?
(How politely they inform you
The pharmacy will close at half-past five.)
Or are you working still?
Patiently advising and assisting
The lost and the inquisitive
The length and breadth of Europe.

Eileen Anne Gordon

Dealing with Monsters

I have become adept at let's pretend,
take comfort in fairy tales
where candles lit in hope
refuse to splutter and die.
I bury myself in books
where ogres are felled.
I am that woman, that man,
active, smart and brave
who triumphs over evil
in a trilogy at most.
I fall asleep to the song of whales,
my fears tightly corralled.

Come dawn I watch the day
creep round the curtains' edge.
It's down to me how much,
how little, I open them
and let in the dark.

Before the Moon

No celestial Turner heavens
but rather,
a gentle westward
slipping of the day,
when the air is spiced
with woodsmoke
and soft glowing windows
twinkle a warm welcome home.

No cumuli to punctuate rich amber hues
but rather,
the day heaving azure sighs
as her eyelids become heavy
and with a rosy wink,
she nods gently,
that sleep time
is upon her.

Aide Memoire

That sticky summer afternoon in France,
when we were so hot, even in the motley shade
of the plum trees – mirabelles, I think they were –
sunlight glancing off the sweet gold sacks falling
into our hands, until we'd eaten enough and idled
down to the river to find the sandy beach where rushes
and tough reeds cluttered the water's edge.

We plunged into ice-water straight from the Tarn.
I swam my few feeble strokes then you lunged at me.
'Dive!' you shouted, dragging me down into weeds,
where a root shot up and snagged my knee.
You swam on upstream; I struggled back to the bank
where I watched the blood flow. I still carry the scar.

Rossini in Skopje

In the haven of September
Rossini came. The city was
churning with swallows, riotous
and tipsy with their spinning,
swirling and crescendo,
and in those migrant days
Rossini swam, a single quaver
in a violin-shaped town,
from scroll and ribs to endpin,
with his music hidden.
Eventually, from memory,
he composed *Péchés de vieillesse*,
singing fondly from far-off,
taking up bow and bridge
and crossing that city's strings.

A Proverbial Example

Any mother's daughter knows how to boil a poison egg.
Any mother's daughter can make a gilt bedstead to lie on.
Give her an inch, and she'll fashion a gruesome tale
from hand-me-down gardening gloves
or a fox-fur stole from the dressing-up.

I feared the fox-fur stole,
the thorns in the fingers of the glove,
I ran a mile from the groans of our midnight grandmother clock,
exchanging moth-infested blankets for continental quilts.
I curdled the yolk of any mother's daughter.
I'm the straw that broke my mother's back.

The Very Grey Area of Suburbain Zebras

Shrouded from my sight
on the dark side of the cul-de-sac

they hid
in flowering cherry nursery rhymes
until my seventh birthday   the day

I first made out their forms
horse-hooves   tails   and manes   and all.
I was afraid

afraid they might fall from their rock-a-bye trees
and flatten me
like the cartoon sinner that I am

so I crossed my heart and hoped to meet the zoo-master
by booking the trip of an afterlife
to Savanna Land   but woe is me

I lost my ticket in the clutter of the kitchen drawer
and that was that, or so I thought.

These days   the ozone sky is wearing thin:
I see their bones   ebony-white as naked angels -
how they shine under wispy skin.

One sundown   I'll surprise these zebras
in their natural habitat.   They'll lift their heads
full stripey   and nuzzle me over the endless plain.

Bridget Khurshead

Last Day in the Mountains

Does the existence of snow really matter?
This patch is old and sunken,

grey and we are not supposed to touch
but we are only human.

We have cycled from the Escorial to see it
grinding through all our gears

and eventually plodding on foot past abandoned
ski station lifts. And at the summit at last

a blob of off-white childish memories.
Ours to plunge our fingers in

throwing snowballs at our shadows
in the melting sun

until cars pass us and we stand up embarrassed.
Ready to test the hairpins

swerving out against gravity again
as if possessed, slick

right to the road edges, we flame down
towards the rocket-like fountains of Idelfonso.

Attic

Now I have this eyeful of sky
And this perch on the roof of the world
This is always what I wanted,
The restful gaze that shines like a sun and
A head that cocks like a sparrow.
Over to my right, the horizon's duty edge
To my left a steep incline of slate reflecting
Bone and a multitude of sins.
I ride the nerve ends of sky like a hawk,
Talons grip my past that beats like
A runner's breath under the safety of wing.
And now the moon comes up with
Its sickly paleness, skirting shadows,
And a cyclop eye on my dominions.

Tennis Lessons

At summer's end I'd search the garden
for lost balls, long-sleeved with your
thick gloves and hat. A whole day's task
to part blue nettles, crawl through shrubs
and tangled roots, lifting every leaf
to find them gone fuzzy and dull
in the damp. Dad, I know
you let me win; your wild aim
had me laughing well past dinner.
I loved your serve, your strong arms
and their long shadows arcing
out but always back, ball flying
in the squint of the sun. I loved
them knocking heavy branches
on our broad-leaved tree, the fat figs
that dropped onto our court. But
when we pitched the old net today
it was the same: your easy loss,
your hits gone rogue, a hopeless aim.

Sujatha Menon

Mimicry in G Minor

It started on the cusp of a semilunar moon,
a migration of pain from coast to coast across
the tundra, where whispers grew wild and tangled
up in the 12 hollows of my throat.
In those scratchy nooks, clutches of
eggs hatched asynchronously
sounding like the flight calls of
old cell phone messages fading
with the sky.
On examination, with the also tangled stethoscope
every thump had a wingbeat and a melodious span
of muffles, clicks and tweets.
It had been a year since the funeral,
since we celebrated with sandwiches
and threw the crusts to birds,
but the days were still long and tapered
towards the night, where bats not stars
helped us to find our way
to the swelling murmuration of
our hearts, also straining to take flight.

Blush

Misty day and the world alive with water.
Some days I track sand and kelp and salt home and
other days the water rushes up the beach to my door and
slaps me in my chest right where I stand.

I can't tell you what I've learned from sickness that
takes root somewhere deep in the body and
becomes the great eclipsing force of your life.
But I can tell you what's on the other side of it.

The victories here are immense – I eat enough and
sleep enough and still speak to my childhood friends.
I don't hate spring anymore – the cherry blossom outside
my window is in the infancy of its mid-March bloom.
Like it, I am learning to blush.

The worst thing about being sick is the loneliness.
The best thing about not being sick is that the
knives have finally left me alone.
They used to be everywhere.
They wanted the soft white skin of my underbelly
but they were satisfied with my eyes.

I wish I had a lesson for you at the end of all this grief.
Something to hand to you with a bow on it
and a box around it. Instead, I have only the long
tenacious grasses that separate the sand
from the concrete and sway this way and that
in the still frigid winds off the sea.

Like them, I am learning to dance.

Flies

I am being followed by a swarm
of flies. Sometimes, the flies are silent,
but never still. Sometimes, I forget
the flies are there, as they are behind me, then I see
the swarm in front of me, hovering over
a puddle, tree stump or stagnant gully. Perhaps
they are merely gnats, black pins, a frenzy, caught between
snags in the wind. I want to make out their kind, yet when
I step closer, the swarm murmurs, swells and rises.
I read of names: march fly, coffin fly, cluster fly, horn fly,
bot fly, scuttle fly, blow fly, flesh fly. In the morning,
the swarm is low, like smoke by my bed, growing
as I move, following as I leave the house, walk the road,
the towpath, the ditch. Most of the time there is a fury,
flying around and around within circles, high
and low. The flies do not speak or tell me why
they are here. I do not know what to feed them, whether
they need sleep, quiet. The swarm makes no shadow
on the ground. I return to dank evenings, tug at threads
attached from me to the flies – the swarm shifting,
turning. I hear flies at night: spurs and bristles grating,
a low-pitched sawing, guzzling. Some days, the swarm loosens,
blue and emerald flies that dart away.

Ansuya Patel

Abecedarian of a Train Journey

Arriving at the platform, I carry a
bag with my grandmother's mango jam,
cartons of pistachio halva,
desi liquor for my friend, Robert. The
engine hums, every seat is taken.
Fields blur past like shadows.
Glimpses of towns I'll never visit.
Hari Rama Hari Krishna echoes
inside the carriage, men in saffron pass.
Juice, chai, vada ! a boy calls out.
Kinetic energy of leaving a place.
Lines from the Gita I recite. A
mother across me holds a baby.
Navsari the town I leave behind.
Over the road a grey cow
ponders existence. I stare ahead,
quiet as the baby's snuffle,
recall my days, collage memories,
someplace my heart dances.
Trivatri, a bunch of girls climb on
unabashed, laugh about their first kiss,
voices of future India and the world. A
wise woman once said *travelling is jatra.*
X-raying every thought and act is for fools.
You're here to unfurl your wings, soar to the
Zenith is what my soul craves.

Geoff Petty

Crank

I know a strange place where they scorn facility,
and embrace the difficult.
When cleaning their teeth, I would expect them to hold the brush still,
and move their heads.

They have half the people making things nobody needs,
and the other half persuading everybody they want them.
When I point this out, they call me a crank.
But they forget their physics,
for without a crank, you will never turn the wheel of progress.

And in this strange place,
they evade the obvious
in their search for their solution.

Should a leader unleash his murderous, raping army
upon a sleeping people,
they talk to the leader,
and kill his army.
I would rather they talked to his army after killing the leader.
But Men weigh the life of one ravenous politician
far heavier than ten thousand virgins
and a forest of felled children.

When I point this out, they call me a clot.
But they forget their biology,
for without clots we would all bleed to death.

(And when I point that out they call me a jerk.
But they forget their sociology,
for you need a jerk, to leave a rut).

Wearing a Poem

I am wearing a poem today.
I'm not sure if I should show it,
Be a peacock, a lark.
A poem tends to fly away, an escapee,
As when a child lets slip a coloured balloon
Believing it will soar forever;
Only mine comes to grief, an Icarus child,
A shot-down drone, drowned. This poem,
I think it fits me perfectly
But you may have different ideas.
You are wondering if it is a brooch or a poppy.
Maybe it's a dress or another form of apparel.
Apparently you have overlooked a necklace.
Would it be blue or jet,
Modern or antique,
Modest or flamboyant?
Intricate, delicate, fetching, distinctive, admirable.
I am giving away no clues
Except to say
I feel wonderful wearing it.
You may give it away, not care for it,
Spoil it like a stain
Splashed up from the gutter.
You may see a different picture,
Dying in the rain, a sodden lump,
To disintegrate, an amorphous mass.
I should give you the benefit of the doubt
But I'm a hesitant poet, a shy poet.
I'd rather bare my body than bare my soul.
So now I'll take off my poem.
It fits inside my soul, waiting.

Metaphor or Lessons Learnt in the Middle of the Night, St Albans

1. Parcel tape has limited effect on an airbed puncture discovered in the dark in a house where the airbed is the only bed.
2. It takes approximately one and half hours for a deflating airbed to deliver its occupants to the polished concrete floor.
3. Males and females react differently to the crisis.
4. The male sleeps noisily and gustily, dreaming of ladders and chickens during the periods between inflations.
5. The female adopts the fight/flight response alternating between visits to the bathroom and making up nasty stories about the airbed.
6. Turning over is ill advised and reminiscent of the periods of moderate to extreme 'chop' experienced on a flight to Boston in 2015.
7. When the bathroom lights also fail the male concludes the airbed has begun a vendetta. The male kicks the airbed. The female whispers they should be careful in case the airbed has feelings.
8. The female, who is a poet, elevates the situation to metaphor but quickly discovers that a deflating airbed is not about identity, ethnicity, the body, sex or climate change. She ignores what it might have to say about gender. She will however always refer to a hiss, whether from a snake or a group of yoga ladies exhaling, as being like an airbed deflating. She will use the simile so often it will become known as her personal cliché and be one of the many reasons why she never wins the T. S Eliot Prize.
9. Mid-afternoon the next day the couple will be careful to avoid conflict over how best to pour milk into tea.
10. Much later they will be found to be suffering from a condition called airbedophobia characterised by the carrying of a puncture repair kit at all times. As the only people publicly admitting to the condition they will be written about at length in the Lancet.

11. The airbed will blame the grit that stabbed it or the men who dragged it or the plastic that surrounded it.
12. The airbed will never say sorry.
13. Even though the airbed is fixed with daubs of PVC glue and a specially designed patch and stays proudly inflated for lengthy periods neither the male nor the female will ever sleep with it again.

Martin Rieser

A Stitch in Time

If I could,
I would force a needle
through Time's thick fabric
to hold back
the consequences
of the letting go,
the savage explosion
after so many years,
of arrests
of questionings,
the deaths.

I would stitch up
old wounds,
broken souls,
and hold their pain
in each hand
so that their demons
were tied to the past,
not to a raging future.

I would stitch up
the fallen schools
the hospitals
and apartments
the olive trees
and the rivers
and put it all back
as it was before.

But no clumsy fingers
or even deft hands
can mend
a torn heart,
a wrecked country,
or history, history.

Gloria Sanders

Drawing Life

I spend the liminal hours deciding
which nude sketches to keep
and which to tear in two,
without knowing or minding which I drew

or which best portrays
the truth of a sinew
reclining on a stool.

The creases of a foot are crumpled into a ragged ball,
the curve of a hip is ripped
with the soft serration of paper being torn
from itself

and on the other side I will notice
a small piece of charcoal, crayon, pencil,
has embedded itself in my hand,

a splinter from the other side of the split
carried forward.

Knowing Nothing

Fixing on the nodding blossom tree,
on the other side of thin glass,
I notice the moment when petals detach,
risk being trampled into clammy tarmac.
Inside, channels of sunlight,
between our facing chairs,
reveal galaxies of gate-crashing dust,
shaming idle hands.

You did not choose me, but I chose you.
Sister Monica reads, scoring frail pages
with a yellowing nail – she enjoys the odd fag,
hidden in her heavy robes.
I imagine her pale, waxy body
untouched under those sable folds.
Mauvish, tight lips covered in spit read on;
her crepe hands clutch the words into her lap.

Mum buys compensatory Slush Puppies
every Friday after class – reminds me
of the confirmation cash I'll receive.
Azure drains as I suck – leaving a cup
of dull ice collapsing in on itself.
Best part of the day gone and I'm still
in my school tie trudging home
whilst my sisters watch The Tube with chips.
She told my mum I was slow.

Jackie Skingley

Chiaroscuro
For Nicola

Imprints carve memory, sharp,
blurred. Sun washed sky, silver
sand between painted toes. Your
footprints beside mine. We swam
among coral where angel fish and
moorish idols glide. We picnicked
at Bandar Jissah, eating hummus,
drinking wine.

Ashen skies weep. Sussex earth
turns to mud. Worms work beneath
my booted feet and gulls screech
overhead. You are dust, a souffle
of air, a caress upon my cheek.
Grief drinks, eats reason. Waves
smash groynes, curl along the
pebble shore.

Jackie Skingley

Muttrah Souq Remembered

Walls of heat, infused with spices,
envelope. A swell of people.
Sandalled feet raise dust.
Men in dishdashas gather.
Women in burqas sweep by,
swooping into gold shops
bulging with bangles and beads,
their bright clothes obscured.

Voices ring out, call, barter.
Muhammed Ali sits at peace
smoking a hubbly bubbly pipe.
His son brings mint tea.
Next door, Azziz burns
frankincense in painted jars,
enticing tourists to buy his wares,
Bahla pots and woven baskets.

Ahmed the silver merchant
feeds sardines to cats wearing
shiny collars, links he fashioned into
chain. He looks up. Smiles.
'Salaam Aleikum Kayfa Haluka?'
His greeting, an invitation to enter
a treasure trove of jewellery,
Necklaces, earrings, sharp khanjars.

Muttrah Souq, mid afternoon, the muezzin
chants 'Allahu Akbar' four times.
Ahmed dons his kumma, bids farewell,
locks up and hurries to pray at the mosque.
Steps away, through a great arch,
lies the sequinned sea. Dolphins leap,
red sailed dhows bob, following routes
of Sinbad to India and the Far East.

Bonxies

climb
climb up above the track, above the shallow rusty hollow
where, rare as rocs
the bonxies splash
preen their feathers clean
and where we've seen hooked-beak
bonxies breaking bone
tearing flesh from scavenged lifeless prey
turn now, away above the burn, climb
up through dreek and foggy bog-pool stink
to where dun birds are slave-powered Viking galleys
below us in the treeless valley.
Pause,
pick,
spring
from wedge of spongy sphagnum to tussock
of rush and sedge, over saluting flags of bog cotton
ruffled by a puff of breeze
over blushed black bog bilberry, climb
above where shiny pearls of crowberry grow
climb through midge and stillness
to – we did not know -
the bonxie breeding ground.
Pause
gaze around
sense disturbance
glimpse of bird ballistic exocet
a sparring spear speeding through quiet enervating air
eye level, swerving at the last
and me, invasive species
overthrown

Rainforest

In a wood, between leaves and sun, crews
of cockatoos brocade a blackthorn-tree.
Fanned by a vagrant breeze they sway, ungainly.
Gathered there for its skirt of forest and fruits, they
circle towards seeds, linger a moment longer
near loquats.

We descend towards the gilded glow of evening
to watch rainbow-parrots embroider pearls of ruby
and emerald over branches, bleak, unclothed.
As the bush strips itself bare in winter, late summer tosses
scraps of hope to nature's feathers, offers flights
of conversation between rosellas and lorikeets,
their futures fragile as dreams, strong
as tropical storms.

Marcus Tickner

Christmas Lights in January

The city's lights have been up since the tail of last year.
These are those same lights that now wink coldly, no longer
quick in the eyes of excited children whose bright worlds
span like whirligigs and leapt like jumping jacks.

This day is cobwebbed with sleek drizzle and the lightstrings
hang limp as over-ripe fruit. Now, too weary to sing
of sharp expectation, they whisper, soft, of endings
and lisp of nothing as much as gaudy, empty things.

8am. Cars pass in the rain-shiny streets. The day lacks
energy. And we too, like remnants of the year, unfold
into this drear. But we know we will wear out the longueur –
the shortest day is spent. Shadows shorten and our lights flare.

Christian Ward

Beetle Translations

1.
Ladybirds infested the bedroom
for weeks after the funeral.
Massed in the corner of the window
frames, they arranged themselves
into your favourite things:
A pair of Ray-Ban wayfarer sunglasses
still wearing a tortoiseshell beetle
pattern. A lit cigar with your indentations.
The polished onyx of rosary beads
bright like a stag beetle's wing case.
Paused every time the door creaked open.

2.
Red-headed cardinal beetles
invaded the garden. Wildfire-brilliant,
they made every bird scream.
Turned the robins into blackbirds
with just a look. Not even the rain
acting as a mediator could stop them.

3.
I spoke prayers to the purple
pendant of a violet ground beetle.
Asked for a few moments
of your hand on mine, some quiet peace.

4.
Deathwatch beetles attacked
your old desk. The knocking sound
became a soothing irony.
The woodwork of my body
inched away every second you were
not here.

5.
I spotted a common cockchafer
hovering around the patio lights.
Its strange orbit reminded me
of the laps you took around
the garden. The clumsy flight
continued nightly while your memory
slowly evaporated like the first dew
I'd been expecting for months.

Judith Wozniak

Johannes Could Turn Oil into Light
after A Lady Writing, Johannes Vermeer

You can see it's my likeness, the highbrow,
straight nose, wide-spaced eyes. I'm smiling
at the sudden quickening of new life.

He'd soothe me with stories. How the ultramarine
of my shift is lapis, mined from the mountains
of Afghanistan, crushed with warmed walnut oil.

How he paints shadows in burnt umber from rust
stained clay. My mantle, yellow ochre, lead white,
a touch of vermillion from finely ground cinnabar.

After six weeks of mourning I'm hounded
by creditors. I've settled arrears with the baker.
The poor man has as many mouths to feed.

I follow the Notary Clerk through the house
as he painstakingly records our possessions.

In the oak chest, inlaid with ebony:
Twenty-one children's shirts
Twenty-eight bonnets
Ten men's ruffs
One yellow satin mantle with a fur trim.

It was my mother's, jonquil velvet,
lined with cream silk. I wish
I'd hidden it away, under the eaves.

Johannes loved the way it slid off my skin.
He would fold his face in the soft fabric
to breathe in the fragrance of me.

The clerk, almost done, intones
in his flat preacher voice:
Two easels
Three palettes
Six panels
Ten canvases
One willow cradle

tucked away
for our boy, stillborn
our last child.

Deadman's Ponds

Rain started
when we paused
by the ponds.
The ponds simmered in
a golden sunset. You told me
someone drowned here
last year. I took extra care
treading on the wet clay and reeds.

I worried at one point that we'd get lost
in the dark. I worried
you'd chuck me into the lake
as a joke
I couldn't be sure.
I'm not a good floater.
I worried I'd follow the deadman's step
I worried that I hadn't learned

How to swim without getting
your hair wet;
How to gaze up at the sun
without squinting.
How to devote
without losing oneself;
How to love
without drowning.

The poets

Philip Bellamy lives in retirement on the Flyde Coast North East England. He worked in academic libraries for 35 years. He won the Artemesia Poetry Competition 2023.

Oxford based **Alice Brooker** was short-listed for the Geoff Stevens Memorial Poetry Prize. Her second collection, *Climate Kid*, will be published in 2024 (Broken Sleep Books). Her work features on Masters programmes in Romania and Italy.

Lesley Cooke lives close to the New Forest. A writer, and practitioner of Bach flower remedies, she is published in SOUTH poetry magazine and a handful of other places to date.

Gary Day is a retired English lecturer and the author of *Literary Criticism: A New History* and *The Story of Drama*. He has been writing poetry most of his life.

Francesca Duffield is a writer and artist living in East Sussex. Her poems feature in the Artemisia Arts 2023 anthology, LISP Anthology 2023, *Bourne to Write*, and *Cross-Currents: Curente la Răscruce 2*.

Claudia Farese is an Italian poet, now living in Madrid with their partner, two cats, and a dog. Their work often explores themes of mental health and nature. This poem marks Claudia's first published piece.

Tessa Foley's first collection *Chalet Between Thick Ears* and follow-up collection *What Sort of Bird are You?* are published by Live Canon. She has since been recognised in several writing competitions and published in many literary publications.

Andrew George lives in London where he works as a barrister. His debut collection, *Milk Round*, was published by Live Canon in 2015. He is chair of the charity Modern Poetry in Translation.

Eileen Anne Gordon lives in Bath. She grew up in Scotland and has lived in England, Ireland and Finland. Her poems have appeared in *Obsessed with Pipework*, *The Friday Poem*, and several anthologies.

Kate Gratton has enjoyed living and studying in Kent most of her life. After many years of teaching the arts, she discovered a corner of France to unleash her inner scribe.

Denise O'Hagan is a Sydney-based editor and poet whose work is published and awarded internationally. Her poetry collection *Anamnesis* was a finalist in the Eric Hoffer Book Award and shortlisted in the Rubery Book Award.

Pam Job lives in Essex. Her poems are widely anthologised.

Ben Keatinge is a Dublin-based Irish writer who won the Patrick Kavanagh Poetry Award in 2022 for 'The Wireless Station'. His poems have appeared in *The Irish Times*, *Poetry Ireland Review* and in several anthologies.

Sue Kindon is based in the French Pyrenees. She has published two pamphlets: *She who pays the piper* (Three Drops Press, 2017) and *Outside, the Box* (4Word Press, 2019). She was runner-up in the 2021 Ginkgo Prize (for Eco-poetry). She sometimes writes in French.

Bridget Khursheed is a poet and geek based in the Scottish Borders. She is a Scottish Book Trust New Writers Award recipient for poetry. Her collection *The Last Days of Petrol* is available from Shearsman Books.

Frank Lowry is a 73-year-old ex-teacher who taught in a mixed comprehensive in a socio-economic deprived area of Merseyside. His interests include the natural world; fly fishing, mountain and birds.

Kristen Mears is a freelance writer and editor based in the Surrey Hills. She graduated with an MA from of the University of Kent and an MA in Creative Writing at the Paris School of Arts and Culture. Her passions include climbing, music, and collecting fountain pens.

Sujatha Menon is a poet, artist and musician based in the Midlands UK. Her third poetry collection *Microscopia* is forthcoming with Pindrop Press. Her portfolio can be viewed at *www.sujathamenon.com*

Mili McCoy grew up in Hong Kong and now lives in Scotland. She loves the ocean, country music, red wine, and of course poetry.

Erica-Jane Morris is a poet based in Milton Keynes, UK. Her work has been shortlisted for the Mairtín Crawford Poetry Award 2024, the Live Canon Pamphlet Competition 2022, and she was a finalist in the Mslexia Poetry Competition 2021. *www.ericajanemorris.co.uk*

Londoner **Ansuya Patel** has been published in *Black in White, Drawn to the Light, Gypsophila, Half Way Down The Stairs, Last Stanza, Rattle* and *Crowstep Journal*. She was short-listed by The Alpine and Aurora Prize. Her pamphlet was highly commended by Erbacce and long-listed at Cerasus in 2024.

Geoff Petty was a Warner Bros recording artist – and still writes songs – then a teacher, then an educational consultant and author of very successful books on how to teach.

Anthony Powers, formerly a doctor in general practice, has a BA (Hons) in English Literature and Creative Writing. Published in magazines and anthologies, he attends monthly poetry evenings in Liverpool and Birkenhead.

Estelle Price is the winner of the 2023 Welshpool Poetry Competition, the 2023 Mairtín Crawford Award, the 2021 Welsh Poetry Competition and the 2018 Book of Kells Prize. She was published in 2022 by Nine Arches Press, Primers 6. She writes from a feminist perspective on her East End past, on ecological themes and on relationships.

Martin Rieser is a poet and visual artist. His interactive installations have been shown worldwide. He won the Hastings Poetry Competition 2021 and is published widely including in *Poetry Review, Write to be Counted, Magma, Poetry Kit, The Alchemy Spoon, Acumen,* among others. He was shortlisted for Frosted Fire 2.

Gloria Sanders is a poet and performer raised in London, of Spanish and Eastern-European Jewish heritage. Her website is *www.gloriasanders.com*

Derek Sellen's poems have been published widely and recognised in numerous competitions. He has twice been Canterbury Festival Poet of the Year and three times winner of O'Bheal (Cork).

Jackie Skingley lives in SW France and co-founded Charente Writers. Her work has been published in *Women's Voices* and *First Awakening* anthologies. She is the author of *High Heels & Beetle Crushers.*

Korrin Smith-Whitehouse is a Northampton-based poet, lecturer in Education, editor of *Public Sector Poetry* journal. Her first collection, *Disaffected* (Written Off publishing) explores the problematic and often abusive nature of teaching and learning.

Sally Spiers started writing during the Covid 19 pandemic. She has had two poems published by the *International Times.* Her poem 'The Knitter' was commended in the Brighton and Hove poetry competition 2023. Her poem 'Imposter Syndrome' won first prize in the Charm Poetry competition 2024.

Sally Stanford lives in Charente where she co-founded Charente Writers. She has been ranked in several international competitions and published in anthologies, including Artemesia Arts' *Colours of the Moon.*

Marcus Tickner is a teacher and Wiltshire poet whose poem 'November was a month' was published in *Colours of the Moon,* the anthology of the 2023 Artemesia Arts poetry competition which was judged by Roger McGough. Marcus also writes poetry for children.

The poems of **Mark Totterdell** have been widely published. His recent collections are *Mollusc* (The High Window Press), long-listed for the 2022 Laurel Prize, and *All the Birds* (Littoral Press, 2023).

Christian Ward was long-listed for the 2023 National Poetry Competition. His poems have appeared in *Free the Verse, Loch Raven Review, The Alchemy Spoon, Drawn to the Light,* and *Underscore* magazine. He won the 2024 London Independent Story Prize for poetry and the 2024 Maria Edgeworth Festival Poetry competition.

Rod Whitworth, born in 1943, has done a number of jobs. He currently works as a medical rôle-player. He lives in Oldham and is still tyrannised by commas.

Glen Wilson, winner of the Seamus Heaney Award for New Writing in 2017, also recently scooped the top prize in the Goldsmith Poetry Competition. Since 2019 he has won competitions with Padraic Fallon Poetry, Slipstream Open Poetry, The Fosseway Writers, These 3 Streams Poetry and the Poetry Kit. His collection *An Experience on the Tongue* (Doire Press) is now out.

Judith Wozniak won first prize in the Hippocrates Poetry Competition, 2020. Her pamphlets *Patient Watching* (2022) and *Case Notes* (2024) are published by The Hedgehog Poetry Press. Her poem 'Artist with a Scapel' appeared in the Artemesia Arts 2023 anthology.

Jill Zhao is an academic living in Bristol. She started writing poems after winning a notebook in a raffle draw at her local poetry open mic night. Her poetry explores the everyday (extra)ordinariness of mind and matter; of the natural world; of human relations; of her life as a woman, a daughter, and an immigrant. Her first-ever poem 'Cheeseboard' won the second prize at Clevedon literary festival 2023.

About the cover illustrator

Currently living in France, René Shoemaker has built a career of painting with dyes to create flowing, colourful work on radiant silk glowing with light. A Fine Arts graduate (BFA) of the University of Georgia, where she worked as a librarian until retirement, René has continued refining her art, and sharing her techniques while discovering new ways to express the world we collectively share. Exhibiting in solo and group shows internationally, René delights in exploring our reality through colour and line. Her solo exhibitions include museums in Georgia and Mississippi, where her work is held in permanent collections.

www.reneshoemaker.com

Photo © Jean-Marc Gargantiel
jmgargantiel.zenfolio.com

Afterword from Artemesia Arts...

It is a pleasure to present this second anthology which celebrates a competition that astounded us with the standard of writing and imagery. These poems intrigue, divert and delight. We are very grateful to our poets and of course to our judge, Matt Harvey. His task was not an easy one but the winning poems speak out with strong voices and the other poems clamour alongside – each giving pleasure in its own way.

We want to say a huge thank you to everyone who entered the competition. It would not exist without you and we hope you will continue to invest your poetic aspirations with us. This year's winner, Glen Wilson, said of the competition: "I love the ethos that Artemesia Arts embodies and it is great to be part of an anthology of such high quality creative work, evidenced by the excellent array of pieces in the shortlist."

Artemesia Arts is evolving into a strong collective of writers and poets who all share a love of the English language. Every September we get together in the medieval village of Treignac for a poetry retreat that has become an important pause in the calendar for all of us. As we approach our fourth year, we look forward to a bright future celebrating poetry and literature.

Sheila Schofield & Kate Rose

www.artemesia-arts.com

www.ingramcontent.com/pod-product-compliance
Lightning Source LLC
Chambersburg PA
CBHW011254040426
42452CB00016B/2805